HOW TO SPOT AN ARTIST

THIS MIGHT GET MESSY

BY DANIELLE KRYSA

PRESTEL

MUNICH • LONDON • NEW YORK

Prestel Verlag, Munich · London · New York 2020
A member of Verlagsgruppe Random House GmbH
Neumarkter Strasse 28 · 81673 Munich

Prestel Publishing Ltd.
16-18 Berners Street
London W1T 3LN

Prestel Publishing
900 Broadway, Suite 603
New York, NY 10003

Library of Congress Cataloging-in-Publication Data

Names: Krysa, Danielle, author.
Title: How to spot an artist: this might get messy / Danielle Krysa.
Description: New York : Prestel Publishing, 2020. | Audience: Ages 5-8 |
  Audience: Grades K-1
Identifiers: LCCN 2020006672 | ISBN 9783791374406 (hardcover)
Subjects: LCSH: Artists--Juvenile literature. | Art--Juvenile literature.
Classification: LCC NX163 .K78 2020 | DDC 700.92--dc23
LC record available at https://lccn.loc.gov/2020006672

A CIP catalogue record for this book is available from the British Library.

Editorial direction: Holly La Due
Design and layout: Danielle Krysa
Production management: Anjali Pala

Verlagsgruppe Random House FSC® N001967
Printed on the FSC®-certified paper

Printed in China

ISBN 978-3-7913-7440-6

www.prestel.com

Author's Acknowledgments

This book was inspired by the countless number of people who've shared their "art kid" experiences with me—the good and the bad! Thank you to Holly La Due (Editor), Anjali Pala (Designer), and Kate Woodrow (Literary Agent) for making my childhood dream, of writing and illustrating a kids' book, come true. And of course, thanks to the amazing boys in my life—my husband Greg and my son Charlie.

OH, THANK GOODNESS YOU HAVE THIS BOOK.

You'll need it if you want to spot a real artist.

You see, no two artists are alike.

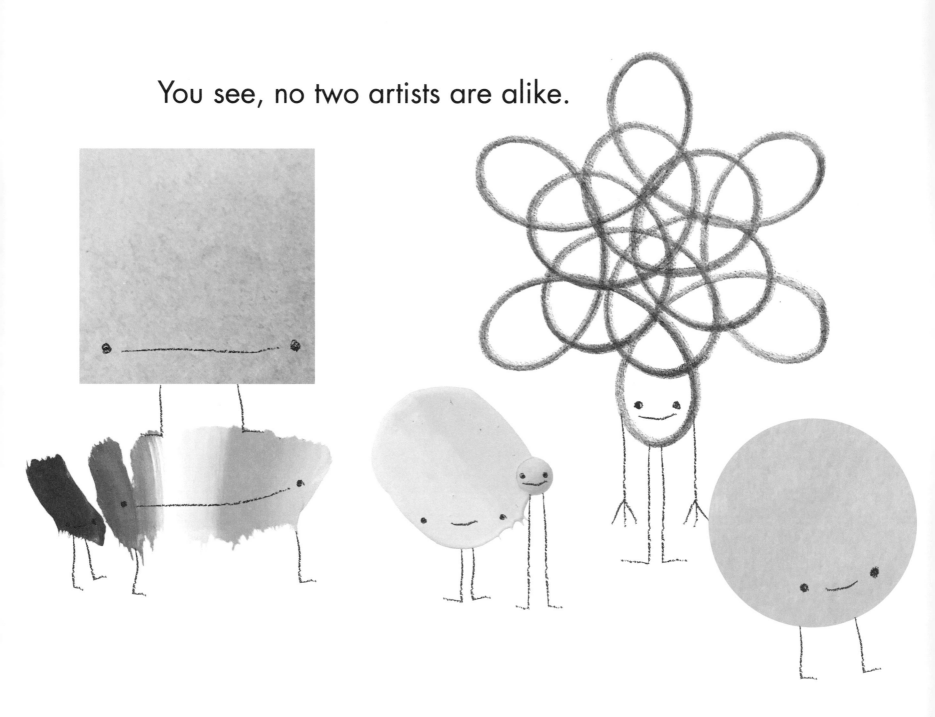

In fact, they come in every size, shape, and color.

 Some are very quiet.

But, they can also be

SUPER LOUD!

There are tidy artists, and others …

not so much.

Artists live in
big, busy cities.

But you can also
find them in teeny
tiny towns out in the
middle of nowhere.

And, to make things even
more complicated …

… they can be any age.

This one, for example,
is ninety-two and a half.

You have to really pay
attention, okay?
Here's what to look for ...

First, artists can often be found turning ordinary stuff—like feathers, rocks, noodles, string, buttons, egg cartons, leaves, and even old socks—into art.

NOTE: GLUE is a very clear (*and sticky*) sign that an artist is nearby.

Magazines full of holes instead of pictures?
Yep, an artist did that.

Parents aren't always thrilled about this, but they need to realize, if pictures don't get cut out, rearranged, and stuck onto other pictures, then the world would never experience wonders like

THE BIRTHDAY CAKE-TUS!

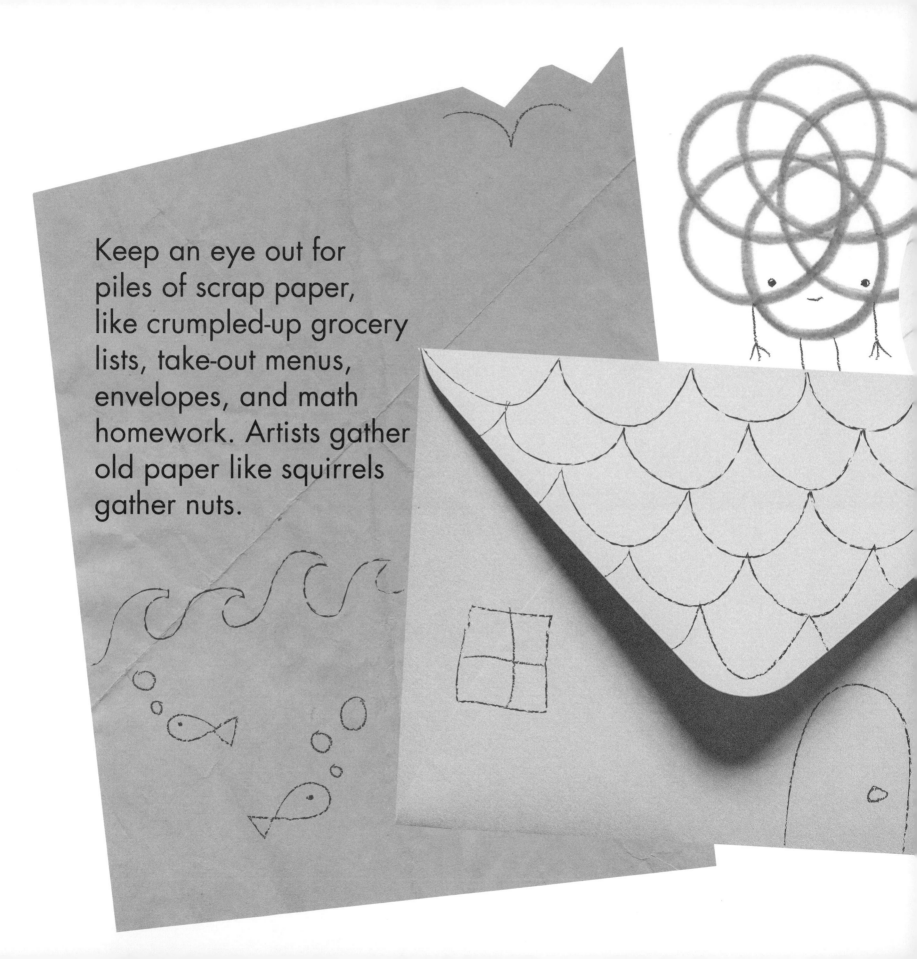

Keep an eye out for piles of scrap paper, like crumpled-up grocery lists, take-out menus, envelopes, and math homework. Artists gather old paper like squirrels gather nuts.

For real, they draw everything on anything.

Oh no …

If you find glitter on the kitchen table, in the fridge, on the cheese, beside the couch, in the bathtub, on the dog—yes, an artist lives here.

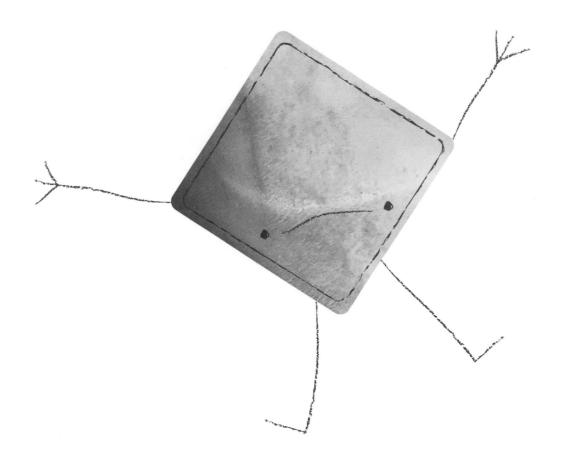

THIS BOOK HAS BEEN INTERRUPTED FOR AN IMPORTANT MESSAGE

This is an art bully.

When this guy shows up, artists can disappear right in front of your eyes. He'll try to replace their artsy ideas with junk like:

YOU CAN'T DO THIS

DON'T SHOW

WHAT A MESS

THAT LOOKS WEIRD

THAT'S NOT PERFECT
ANYBODY
JUST QUIT

If an artist believes any of that **NONSENSE**, the specialness that makes them special starts to fade. They put their pencils down and, eventually, all of their colorful, crazy, wonderful ideas are replaced with ...

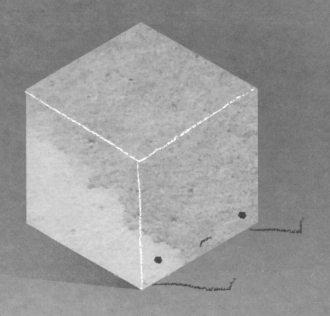

… a quiet, lonely, gray **BLOCK**.

The end.

DDING!

That is not even close to
the end of the story!

This problem can get fixed
in one simple step …

mAKe STUFF

Yes, it's true!
Every time an artist keeps making,
whether it's a mess or a masterpiece,
another rude art bully gets erased.

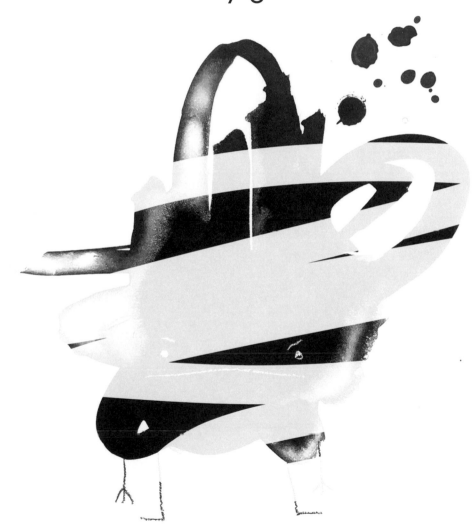

WARNING COMPLETE
Thank you, please continue reading.

Wow. That guy sounds
like a real troublemaker.

Anyway, where were we?
Oh yes, spotting artists.

You now know
what to look
for, but where
should you start
when they could
very well be
ANYWHERE?

EASY!

To see an artist in action, just shout out a bunch of project ideas. Here, try these:

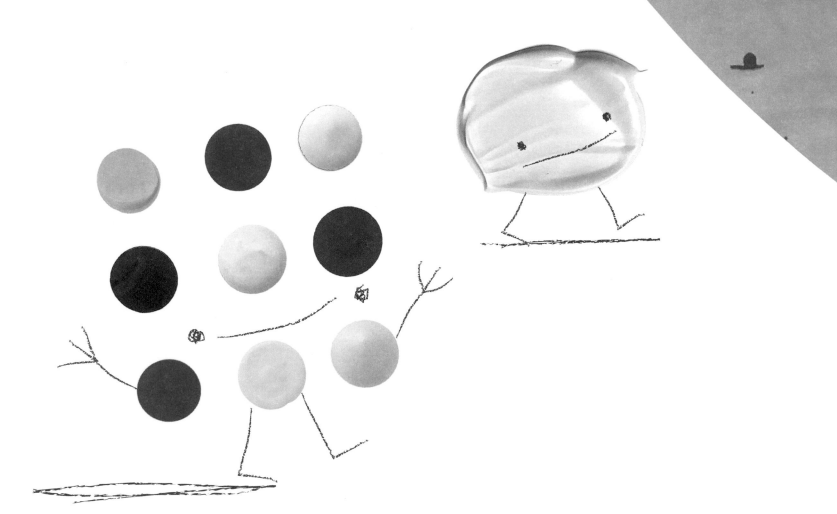

PAINT AN ICE CREAM VOLCANO!

WRITE YOUR NAME WITH ANIMAL LETTERS!

DRAW CRAZY FLOWERS WITH GOOGLY EYES!

Seriously, they'll be making stuff before you can finish reading this book.

If you see grown-ups doing projects like this too, **DO NOT** be alarmed.

They're just like artsy kids, but with really long legs—and jobs.

Yes, artsy kids grow into:

PAINTERS, SCULPTORS, CERAMICISTS, PHOTOGRAPHERS, ART TEACHERS, ILLUSTRATORS, UNIVERSITY PROFESSORS, GRAPHIC DESIGNERS, ARCHITECTS, INTERIOR DESIGNERS, MUSEUM CURATORS, GALLERY OWNERS, MOVIE DIRECTORS, SET DESIGNERS, COSTUME DESIGNERS, COMIC BOOK ARTISTS, ANIMATORS, VIDEO GAME DESIGNERS … oh dear, I was afraid this would happen. This list is too long, and it just keeps going and going, but we are officially out of room. Too. Many. Art. Jobs.

So, there you have it. If you follow every tip and trick in this book, you'll spot an artist in no time.

GOOD LUCK!

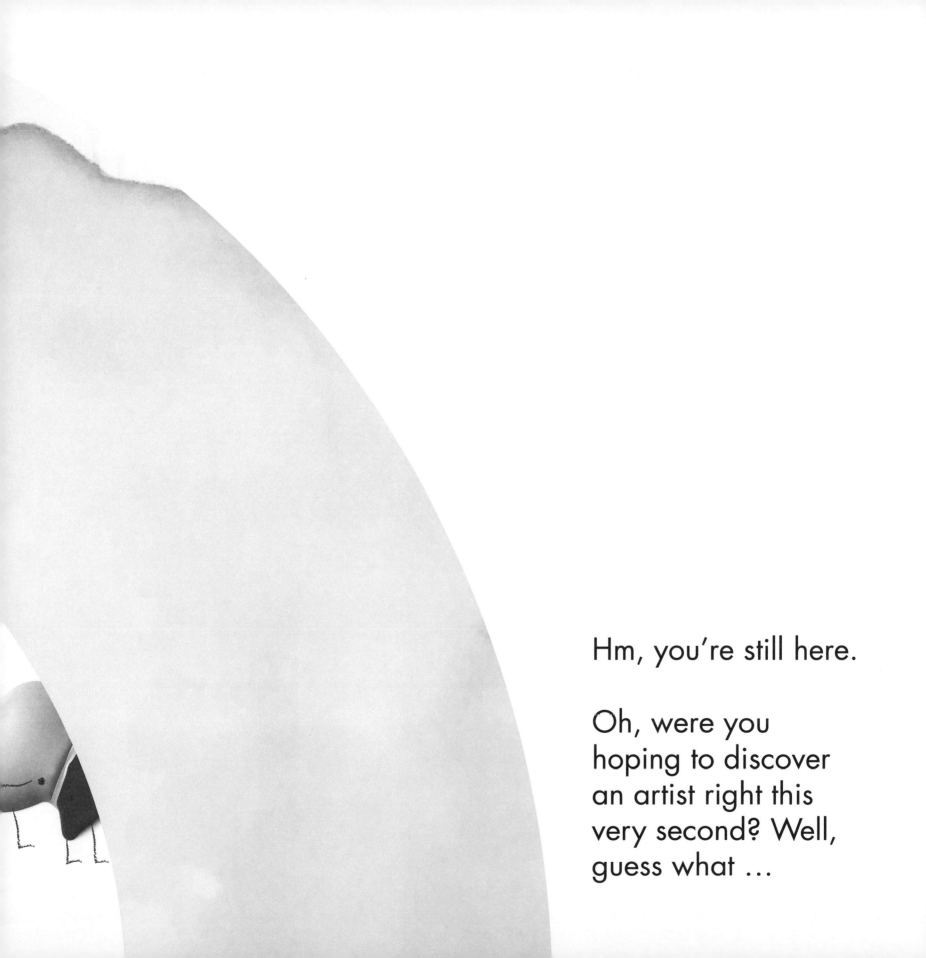

Hm, you're still here.

Oh, were you hoping to discover an artist right this very second? Well, guess what ...

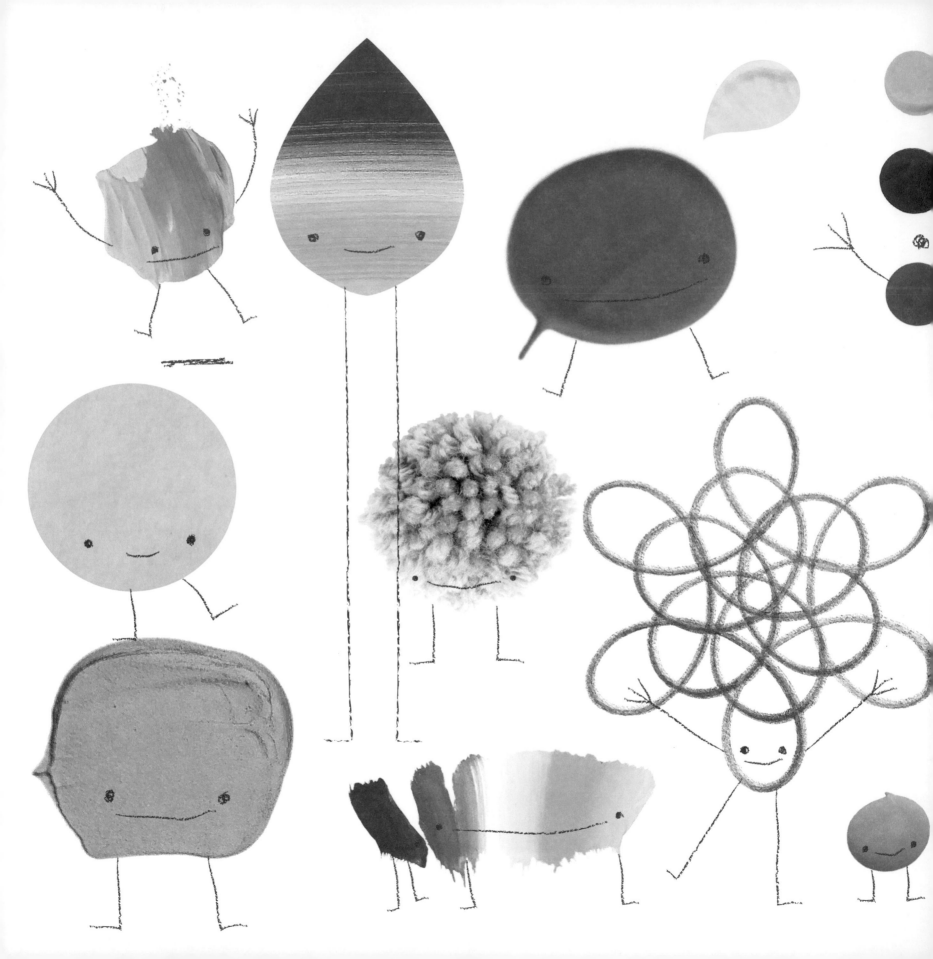

… there's an artist looking at this page

RIGHT
NOW.

More **ART PROJECTS**, because who wants less art projects?

What's your favorite color? What color(s) is the shirt you're wearing? What color is your favorite ice cream? What color is your bedroom? What color are your eyes? Make your own rainbow using all of those colorful answers. Use crayons, paint, cut paper, anything!

Draw a square. Add eyes and a funny hat. Draw a small circle beside your square, with tiny eyes, a big mouth, and some animal ears. Perfect, your square has a weird pet! Name them, then fill everything in with your favorite colors. Done ... well, until the next time you draw a square.

Crisscross lines of tape all over a canvas, or, stick the tape down to look like tree branches, a face, a unicorn - whatever your brilliant brain imagines. Paint over everything with a bunch of colors. When the paint is dry, carefully peel the tape off ... ta-dah, **ART!**

Go outside. Find a rock. Come inside and paint that rock. Go back outside. Leave the rock in a place where someone else can find it to take home and love forever. Do it again.

They say "don't play with your food," but they didn't say anything about making art with it! Every morning arrange bits of your breakfast into a face, ask a grown-up to take a picture of your creation, and then **EAT YOUR BREAKFAST!**

Your mac 'n' cheese is about to become jewelry. Use paint or markers to decorate a pile of uncooked noodles. Once they're dry, choose a colorful piece of string to thread through each new "bead." Hello, fancy necklace.

Raid the recycle bin for old envelopes and magazines. Open the flap of the envelope to make a pointy roof, and decorate the front with windows, a door, or whatever you like. And, so that the house isn't empty, fill the envelope with people cut out of the magazines!

Make a perfectly-not-perfect drawing of yourself. Look in a mirror and draw what you see ... without looking at your paper, and without lifting your pencil off of the page. Seriously. It will be a true **MESS-TERPIECE!** Frame it, put it up in your room, and always be proud that **YOU ARE AN ARTIST.**